The Graduate's Book

The Graduate's Book

Devotions to Guide Your Journey

Scripture quotations are taken from:

The Holy Bible, New International Version (NIV) Copyright © 1973, 1978, 1984, by International Bible Society. Used by permission of Zondervan Publishing House. All rights reserved.

The Holy Bible, New King James Version (NKJV) Copyright © 1982 by Thomas Nelson, Inc. Used by permission.

The Holy Bible, New Living Translation (NLT) Copyright © 1996. Used by permission of Tyndale House Publishers, Incorporated, Wheaton, Illinois 60189. All rights reserved.

The New American Standard Bible®, (NASB) Copyright © 1960, 1962, 1963, 1968, 1971, 1972, 1973, 1975, 1977, 1995 by The Lockman Foundation. Used by permission.

The Holman Christian Standard Bible™ (HCSB) Copyright © 1999, 2000, 2001 by Holman Bible Publishers. Used by permission.

Cover Design by Kim Russel
Page Layout by Bart Dawson

ISBN 1-4041-8432-5

Printed in the United States of America

Table of Contents

How to Use This Book

Because you are reading a book with the word "graduate's" in its title, it's likely that congratulations are in order. If you have recently graduated, please accept a metaphorical pat on the back. You've earned it.

Now that your alma mater is a topic to be discussed in the past tense, you may be facing many decisions: where to live, where to work, and what to do about your personal relationships. These decisions are important, of course, but they are insignificant when compared to a single overriding choice that will fashion your eternal destiny. That decision is your commitment to form a personal, saving relationship with Jesus Christ.

Perhaps you have heard the old saying, "First you make your habits, and then your habits make you." It's true: the habits you form will, to a surprising extent, determine the person you become. No habit is more important to your spiritual growth than the discipline of daily prayer and devotion to God, and this little book is intended to help.

This text is divided into 31 chapters, one

for each day of the month. During the next 31 days, read a chapter each day. If you're already committed to a daily worship time, this book will enrich that experience. If you are not, the simple act of giving God a few minutes each morning will change the tone and direction of your life.

You've put in lots of hard work in order to earn your degree, and you are about to embark upon the journey of a lifetime. If you make every step of that journey with Christ by your side—and if you build your faith upon the firm foundation of God's promises—you will claim for yourself the abundance and grace that God intends for your life. So today, if you do nothing else, accept God's grace with open arms. When you do, you will be the proud recipient of a priceless gift that will change your life forever and endure throughout eternity.

Your Journey
with Christ

For I am persuaded, that neither death,
nor life, nor angels, nor principalities, nor
powers, nor things present, nor things to come,
nor height, nor depth, nor any other creature,
shall be able to separate us from the love of
God, which is in Christ Jesus our Lord.
Romans 8:38-39 KJV

How much does Christ love us? More than we, as mere mortals, can comprehend. His love is perfect and steadfast. Even though we are fallible and wayward, the Good Shepherd cares for us still. Even though we have fallen far short of the Father's commandments, Christ loves us with a power and depth that is beyond our understanding. The sacrifice that Jesus made upon the cross was made for each of us, and His love endures to the edge of eternity and beyond.

Christ's love changes everything. When you accept His gift of grace, you are transformed not only for today, but also for all eternity. Yes, Christ's love changes everything. If you haven't already done so, accept Jesus Christ as Your Savior. He's waiting patiently for you to invite Him into your heart. Please don't make Him wait a single minute longer.

Major on Jesus Christ. Make Him
the preeminent One in your life. You have
all things in Him, with Him, and through
Him—and nothing is greater than that.
Warren Wiersbe

Being a Christian means accepting the terms
of creation, accepting God as our Maker and
Redeemer, and growing day by day into
an increasingly glorious creature in Christ,
developing joy, experiencing love,
maturing in peace.
Eugene Peterson

You're in a hurry. God is not. Trust God.
Marie T. Freeman

Jesus Christ is the same yesterday
and today and forever.
Hebrews 13:8 NASB

A Prayer for the Journey

Heavenly Father, I praise You for Your Son.
Jesus is my Savior and my strength.
Let me share His Good News with all who
cross my path, and let me share His love
with all who need His healing touch.

— Amen —

Faith for the
Journey

But Jesus turned him about, and when
he saw her, he said, Daughter, be of good
comfort; thy faith hath made thee whole. And
the woman was made whole from that hour.
Matthew 9:22 KJV

H ave you ever felt your faith in God slipping away? If so, you are not alone. Every life—including yours—is a series of successes and failures, celebrations and disappointments, joys and sorrows. But even when we feel very distant from God, God is never distant from us.

Jesus taught His disciples that if they had faith, they could move mountains. You can too. When you place your faith, your trust, indeed your life in the hands of Christ Jesus, you'll be amazed at the marvelous things He can do with you and through you. So strengthen your faith through praise, through worship, through Bible study, and through prayer. And trust God's plans. With Him, all things are possible, and He stands ready to open a world of possibilities for you if you have faith.

Faith is two empty hands held open
to receive all of the Lord Jesus.
Alan Redpath

Faith in faith is pointless. Faith in a living,
active God moves mountains.
Beth Moore

Faith is not a feeling; it is action.
It is a willed choice.
Elisabeth Elliot

Anything is possible if a person believes.
Mark 9:23 NLT

A Prayer for the Journey

Dear Lord, make me Your obedient,
faithful servant. You are with me always.
Give me faith and let me remember that with
Your love and Your power, I can live
courageously and faithfully
today and every day.
— Amen —

Courage for the Journey

But He said to them, "Why are you fearful,
O you of little faith?" Then He arose and
rebuked the winds and the sea,
and there was a great calm.
Matthew 8:26 NKJV

A storm rose quickly on the Sea of Galilee, and the disciples were afraid. Although they had seen Jesus perform many miracles, the disciples feared for their lives, so they turned to their Savior, and He calmed the waters and the wind.

Sometimes, we, like the disciples, feel threatened by the inevitable storms of life. And when we are fearful, we, too, can turn to Christ for courage and for comfort.

The next time you're afraid, remember that the One who calmed the wind and the waves is also your personal Savior. And remember that the ultimate battle has already been won at Calvary. We, as believers, can live courageously in the promises of our Lord . . . and we should.

When once we are assured that God is good,
then there can be nothing left to fear.
Hannah Whitall Smith

Down through the centuries, in times
of trouble and trial, God has brought courage
to the hearts of those who love Him. The Bible
is filled with assurances of God's help and
comfort in every kind of trouble which might
cause fears to arise in the human heart. You
can look ahead with promise, hope, and joy.
Billy Graham

I sought the LORD, and he heard me,
and delivered me from all my fears.
Psalm 34:4 KJV

A Prayer for the Journey

Dear Lord, let me turn to You for courage
and for strength. When I am fearful, keep me
mindful of Your promises. When I am anxious,
let me turn my thoughts and prayers to
the priceless gift of Your Son. You are with
me always, Heavenly Father, and I will face
the challenges of this day with
trust and assurance in You.

— Amen —

Trusting God's Promises

Trust in the LORD with all your heart,
and lean not on your own understanding;
in all your ways acknowledge Him,
and He shall direct your paths.

Proverbs 3:5-6 NKJV

God's promises are found in a book like no other: the Holy Bible. The Bible is a roadmap for life here on earth and for life eternal. As Christians, we are called upon to trust its promises, to follow its commandments, and to share its Good News.

As believers, we must study the Bible daily and meditate upon its meaning for our lives. Otherwise, we deprive ourselves of a priceless gift from our Creator. God's Holy Word is, indeed, a transforming, life-changing, one-of-a-kind treasure. And, a passing acquaintance with the Good Book is insufficient for Christians who seek to obey God's Word and to understand His will.

God has made promises to mankind and to you. God's promises never fail and they never grow old. You must trust those promises and share them with your family, with your friends, and with the world.

You will be able to trust Him only to
the extent that you know Him!
Kay Arthur

Trust in yourself and you are doomed
to disappointment; trust in money and you may
have it taken from you, but trust in God,
and you are never to be confounded
in time or eternity.
D. L. Moody

Trusting God is the bottom line
of Christian righteousness.
R. C. Sproul

Commit everything you do to the LORD.
Trust him, and he will help you.
Psalm 37:5 NLT

A Prayer for the Journey

Lord, Your Holy Word contains promises,
and I will trust them. I will use the Bible as my
guide, and I will trust You, Lord, to speak to
me through Your Holy Spirit and through
Your Holy Word, this day and forever.
— Amen —

And the Greatest of These

But now abide faith, hope, love, these three;
but the greatest of these is love.
1 Corinthians 13:13 NASB

The familiar words of 1 Corinthians 13 remind us that love is God's commandment. Faith is important, of course. So, too, is hope. But, love is more important still. However, we sometimes, despite our best intentions, fail to obey our Lord. When we become embittered with ourselves, with our neighbors, or most especially with God, we disobey the One who gave His life for us.

Christ showed His love for us on the cross, and, as Christians, we are called upon to return Christ's love by sharing it. Today, let us spread Christ's love to families, friends, and strangers by our words and our deeds.

In the presence of love, miracles happen.
Robert Schuller

Since God is perfect in loving man,
man must be perfect in loving his neighbor.
Vincent Pallotti

There is nothing that makes us love someone
so much as praying for them.
William Law

Above all, love each other deeply, because
love covers over a multitude of sins.
1 Peter 4:8 NIV

A Prayer for the Journey

Lord, love is Your commandment.
Help me always to remember that the gift
of love is a precious gift indeed. Let me
nurture love and treasure it. And, keep me
mindful that the essence of love is not to
receive it, but to give it, today and forever.
— Amen —

The
Abundant Life

I have come that they may have life,
and that they may have it more abundantly.
John 10:10 NKJV

The tenth chapter of John tells us that Christ came to earth so that our lives might be filled with abundance. But what, exactly, did Jesus mean when He promised "life . . . more abundantly"? Was Jesus referring to material possessions or financial wealth? Hardly. When Jesus declared Himself the shepherd of mankind (John 10:7-9), He offered a different kind of abundance: a spiritual richness that extends beyond the temporal boundaries of this world.

The fullness of life in Christ is available to all who seek it and claim it. Count yourself among that number. Seek first the salvation available through a personal relationship with Jesus Christ, and then claim the joy, the peace, and the spiritual abundance that the Shepherd offers His sheep.

God loves you and wants you to experience
peace and life—abundant and eternal.
Billy Graham

God is the giver, and we are the receivers.
And His richest gifts are bestowed
not upon those who do the greatest things,
but upon those who accept His abundance
and His grace.
Hannah Whitall Smith

People, places, and things were never meant
to give us life. God alone is
the author of a fulfilling life.
Gary Smalley & John Trent

And God will generously provide all you need.
Then you will always have everything you
need and plenty left over to share with others.
2 Corinthians 9:8 NLT

A Prayer for the Journey

Thank You, Father, for the abundant life
that is mine through Christ Jesus. Guide me
according to Your will, and help me to be
a worthy servant through all that I say and do.
Give me courage, Lord, to claim the rewards
You have promised, and when I do,
let all the glory be Yours.
— Amen —

Do Unto Others . . .

Therefore, whatever you want men to do
to you, do also to them,
for this is the Law and the Prophets.
Matthew 7:12 NKJV

How should we treat other people? God's Word is clear: We should treat others in the same way that we wish to be treated. This Golden Rule is easy to understand, but sometimes it can be difficult to live by.

Because we are imperfect human beings, we are, on occasion, selfish, thoughtless, or cruel. But God commands us to behave otherwise. He teaches us to rise above our own imperfections and to treat others with unselfishness and love. When we observe God's Golden Rule, we help build His kingdom here on earth. And, when we share the love of Christ, we share a priceless gift; may we share it today and every day that we live.

Good will is written into the constitution
of things; ill will is sand in the machinery.
E. Stanley Jones

Let Christ be formed in me, and let me learn
of Him all lowliness of heart, all gentleness
of bearing, all modesty of speech,
all helpfulness of action, and promptness
in the doing of my Father's will.
John Baillie

If we have the true love of God in our hearts,
we will show it in our lives. We will not have
to go up and down the earth proclaiming it.
We will show it in everything we say or do.
D. L. Moody

Do to others as you would have them do to you.
Luke 6:31 NIV

A Prayer for the Journey

Dear Lord, let me treat others as I wish
to be treated. Because I expect kindness,
let me be kind. Because I wish to be loved,
let me be loving. Because I need forgiveness,
let me be merciful. In all things, Lord, let me
live by the Golden Rule, and let me teach that
rule to others through my words and my deeds.

— Amen —

A Thankful Heart

Enter into His gates with thanksgiving,
And into His courts with praise. Be thankful
to Him, and bless His name. For the LORD
is good; His mercy is everlasting,
And His truth endures to all generations.
Psalm 100:4-5 NKJV

As believing Christians, we are blessed beyond measure. God sent His only Son to die for our sins. And, God has given us the priceless gifts of eternal love and eternal life. We, in turn, are instructed to approach our Heavenly Father with reverence and thanksgiving. But sometimes, in the crush of everyday living, we simply don't stop long enough to pause and thank our Creator for the countless blessings He has bestowed upon us.

When we slow down and express our gratitude to the One who made us, we enrich our own lives and the lives of those around us. Thanksgiving should become a habit, a regular part of our daily routines. God has blessed us beyond measure, and we owe Him everything, including our eternal praise.

Thank God every morning when you get up
that you have something to do that day which
must be done, whether you like it or not.
Charles Kingsley

We should spend as much time
in thanking God for His benefits
as we do asking Him for them.
St. Vincent de Paul

God is worthy of our praise and is pleased
when we come before Him with thanksgiving.
Shirley Dobson

I will give thanks to the LORD with all
my heart; I will tell of all Your wonders.
I will be glad and exult in You;
I will sing praise to Your name, O Most High.
Psalm 9:1-2 NASB

A Prayer for the Journey

Heavenly Father, Your gifts are greater than
I can imagine. May I live each day with
thanksgiving in my heart and praise on my
lips. Thank You for the gift of Your Son and
for the promise of eternal life. Let me share
the joyous news of Jesus Christ, and let my life
be a testimony to His love and to His grace.

— Amen —

Sharing the
Good News

Go therefore and make disciples of all
the nations, baptizing them in the name of
the Father and of the Son and of
the Holy Spirit, teaching them to observe
all things that I have commanded you;
and lo, I am with you always,
even to the end of the age.
Matthew 28:19-20 NKJV

The Good News of Jesus Christ should be shouted from the rooftops by believers the world over. But all too often, it is not. For a variety of reasons, many Christians keep their beliefs to themselves, and when they do, the world suffers because of their failure to speak up.

Paul shared a message to believers of every generation when he wrote, "God has not given us a spirit of timidity" (2 Timothy 1:7 NASB). Paul's meaning is clear: When sharing our testimonies, we must be courageous, forthright, and unashamed. As believers in Christ, we know how He has touched our hearts and changed our lives. Now is the time to share our personal testimonies with others.

The old familiar hymn begins, "What a friend we have in Jesus . . . ." No truer words were ever penned. Jesus is the sovereign friend and ultimate savior of mankind. Christ showed enduring love for His believers by willingly sacrificing His own life so that we might have eternal life. Let us love Him, praise Him, and share His message of salvation with our neighbors and with the world.

In their heart of hearts, I think all true followers of Christ long to become contagious Christians. Though unsure about how to do so or the risks involved, deep down they sense that there isn't anything as rewarding as opening a person up to God's love and truth.

Bill Hybels

Witnessing is not something that we do for the Lord; it is something that He does through us if we are filled with the Holy Spirit.

Warren Wiersbe

We are therefore Christ's ambassadors, as though God were making his appeal through us. We implore you on Christ's behalf: Be reconciled to God.

2 Corinthians 5:20 NIV

A Prayer for the Journey

Dear Lord, let me share the Good News
of Your Son Jesus. Let the life that I live and
the words that I speak bear testimony to
my faith in Him. And let me share the story
of my salvation with others so that they, too,
might dedicate their lives to Christ
and receive His eternal gifts.

— Amen —

A Life of Righteousness and Obedience

Now by this we know that we know Him,
if we keep His commandments.
1 John 2:3 NKJV

Since God created Adam and Eve, we human beings have been rebelling against our Creator. Why? Because we are unwilling to trust God's Word, and we are unwilling to follow His commandments. God has given us a guidebook for righteous living called the Holy Bible. It contains thorough instructions that, if followed, lead to fulfillment, righteousness and salvation. But, if we choose to ignore God's commandments, the results are as predictable as they are tragic.

Talking about God is easy; living by His commandments is considerably harder. But, unless we are willing to abide by God's laws, all of our righteous proclamations ring hollow. How can we best proclaim our love for the Lord? By obeying Him. And, for further instructions, read the manual.

Obedience is the key of knowledge.
Christina Rossetti

A life of obedience is not a life of following
a list of do's and don'ts, but it is allowing
God to be original in our lives.
Vonette Z. Bright

Nobody is good by accident.
No man ever became holy by chance.
C. H. Spurgeon

If they obey and serve him, they will spend
the rest of their days in prosperity
and their years in contentment.
Job 36:11 NIV

A Prayer for the Journey

Dear Lord, this world is filled with so many
temptations, distractions, and frustrations.
When I turn my thoughts away from You
and Your Word, I suffer. But when I turn
my thoughts, my faith, and my prayers to You,
I am safe. Direct my path, Father,
and let me discover Your will for
today and for all eternity.
— Amen —

God's Love for the Journey

You are my God, and I will give you thanks;
you are my God, and I will exalt you.
Give thanks to the LORD, for he is good;
his love endures forever.
Psalm 118:28-29 NIV

God loves our world so much that He sent His only begotten Son to die for our sins. How blessed we are to have received God's miraculous gift.

God is a loving Father. We are God's children, and we are called upon to be faithful to Him. We return our Father's love by sharing it with others. We honor our Heavenly Father by obeying His commandments and sharing His message. When we do, we are blessed . . . and the Father smiles.

God loves us the way we are, but He loves us
too much to leave us that way.
Leighton Ford

God is a God of unconditional, unremitting
love, a love that corrects and chastens
but never ceases.
Kay Arthur

Jesus loves us with fidelity, purity, constancy,
and passion, no matter how imperfect we are.
Stormie Omartian

We know how much God loves us,
and we have put our trust in him. God is love,
and all who live in love live in God,
and God lives in them.
1 John 4:16 NLT

A Prayer for the Journey

Lord, Your love is infinite and eternal.
Although I cannot fully understand the depths
of Your love, I can praise it, return it,
and share it . . . today and every day.
— Amen —

Discipline for the Journey

Discipline yourself for the purpose
of godliness.
1 Timothy 4:7 NASB

Students everywhere understand the profound sense of joy that accompanies two little words: "School's out!" In a brief, two-word exclamatory sentence, so much is said. "School's out!" means no more homework, no more papers, no more grades, and no more standardized tests. "School's out!" means it's time to put the books—and the worries— away. But before the celebration gets out of hand, be forewarned: "School's out!" does not mean that our work is done. To the contrary, the real work is probably just beginning.

Those who study the Bible are confronted again and again with God's intention that His children lead disciplined lives. God doesn't reward laziness. To the contrary, He expects us to work diligently *before* we reap a bountiful harvest, not after.

As a recent graduate, you've earned the right to proclaim "School's out!" at the top of your lungs. And then, when all the shouting is over, remember that God rewards discipline just as certainly as He punishes slothfulness. And if you're not sure what the word *sloth* means, then school isn't really out yet, now is it? Your dictionary is in that stack of books over there in the corner. Happy reading!

Regardless of how busy we become with all things Christian, we must remember that the most transforming practice available to us is the disciplined intake of Scripture.
Donald S. Whitney

God cannot build character without our cooperation. If we resist Him, then He chastens us into submission. But, if we submit to Him, then He can accomplish His work. He is not satisfied with a halfway job. God wants a perfect work; He wants a finished product that is mature and complete.
Warren Wiersbe

He who heeds discipline shows the way to life, but whoever ignores correction leads others astray.
Proverbs 10:17 NIV

A Prayer for the Journey

Dear Lord, thank You for the gift of Your Son
Jesus, my personal Savior. Let me be a worthy
disciple of Christ, and let me be ever grateful
for His love. I offer my life to You, Lord,
so that I might live according to Your
commandments and according to Your plan.
I will praise You always as I give thanks for
Your Son and for Your everlasting love.
— Amen —

Friends for the
Journey

A friend loves at all times.
Proverbs 17:17 NIV

Loyal Christian friendship is ordained by God. Throughout the Bible, we are reminded to love one another, to care for one another, and to treat one another as we wish to be treated. As you journey through the day ahead, remember the important role that Christian friendship plays in God's plans for His kingdom and for your life.

Today, resolve to be a trustworthy, encouraging, loyal friend. And, treasure the people in your life who are loyal friends to you.

Christ promises His followers that through Him they may experience abundance (John 10:10). May your friends bless you abundantly, and may you do the same for them.

A friend is one who makes me do my best.
Oswald Chambers

The best times in life are made a thousand
times better when shared with a dear friend.
Luci Swindoll

No receipt opens the heart but a true friend,
to whom you may impart griefs, joys,
fears, hopes, suspicions, counsels,
and whatever lies upon the heart.
Francis Bacon

As iron sharpens iron,
a friend sharpens a friend.
Proverbs 27:17 NLT

A Prayer for the Journey

Lord, thank You for my friends.
Let me be a trustworthy friend to others,
and let my love for You be reflected
in my genuine love for them.
— Amen —

In Times of Adversity

In this world you will have trouble.
But take heart! I have overcome the world.
John 16:33 NIV

From time to time, all of us have to face troubles and disappointments. When we do, God stands ready to protect us. Psalm 147 promises, "He heals the brokenhearted" (v. 3 NIV), but it doesn't say that He heals them instantly. Usually, it takes time for God to heal His children.

If you find yourself in any kind of trouble, pray about it and ask God for help. And then be patient. God will work things out, just as He has promised, but He will do it in His own time and according to His own plan.

Are you anxious? Take those anxieties to God. Are you troubled? Take your troubles to Him. Does your world seem to be trembling beneath your feet? Seek protection from the One who cannot be moved. The same God who created the universe will protect you if you ask Him . . . so ask Him.

God doesn't always change the circumstances,
but He can change us to meet
the circumstances. That's what it means
to live by faith.
Warren Wiersbe

It is the trial of our faith that is precious.
If we go through the trial, there is so much
wealth laid up in our heavenly bank account
to draw upon when the next test comes.
Oswald Chambers

Earth has no sorrow that Heaven cannot heal.
St. Thomas More

The righteous face many troubles,
but the LORD rescues them from
each and every one.
Psalm 34:19 NLT

A Prayer for the Journey

Dear Heavenly Father, You are my strength
and my protector. When I am troubled,
You comfort me. When I am discouraged, You
lift me up. When I am afraid, You deliver me.
Let me turn to You, Lord, when I am weak.
In times of adversity, let me trust Your plan
and Your will for my life. Your love is infinite,
as is Your wisdom. Whatever my
circumstances, Dear Lord, let me always
give the praise, and the thanks,
and the glory to You.
— Amen —

Praise for the Father

Praise the LORD. Give thanks to the LORD,
for he is good; his love endures forever.
Psalm 106:1 NIV

When is the best time to praise God? In church? When we tuck little children into bed? Before dinner is served? None of the above. The best time to praise God is all day, every day, to the greatest extent we can, with thanksgiving in our hearts.

Too many of us, even well-intentioned believers, tend to "compartmentalize" our waking hours into a few familiar categories: work, rest, play, family time, and worship. To do so is a mistake. Worship and praise should be woven into the fabric of everything we do; it should never be relegated to a weekly three-hour visit to church on Sunday morning.

Mrs. Charles E. Cowman, the author of the classic devotional text *Streams in the Desert*, wrote, "Two wings are necessary to lift our souls toward God: prayer and praise. Prayer asks. Praise accepts the answer." Today, find a little more time to lift your concerns to God in prayer, and praise Him for all that He has done. He's listening . . . and He wants to hear from you.

Praise and thank God for who He is
and for what He has done for you.
Billy Graham

Today you will encounter God's creation.
When you see the beauty around you, let each
detail remind you to lift your head in praise.
Max Lucado

Preoccupy my thoughts with
your praise beginning today.
Joni Eareckson Tada

Let my mouth be filled with thy praise
and with thy honor all the day.
Psalm 71:8 KJV

A Prayer for the Journey

Lord, Your hand created the smallest grain of sand and the grandest stars in the heavens. You watch over Your entire creation, and You watch over me. Thank You, Lord, for loving this world so much that You sent Your Son to die for our sins. Let me always be grateful for the priceless gift of Your Son, and let me praise Your holy name forever.

— Amen —

Using Our Talents

I remind you to fan into flame the gift of God.
2 Timothy 1:6 NIV

The old saying is both familiar and true: "What we are is God's gift to us; what we become is our gift to God." Each of us possesses special talents, gifted by God, that can be nurtured carefully or ignored totally. Our challenge, of course, is to use our abilities to the greatest extent possible and to use them in ways that honor our Savior.

Are you using your natural talents to make God's world a better place? If so, congratulations. But if you have gifts that you have not fully explored and developed, perhaps you need to have a chat with the One who gave you those gifts in the first place. Your talents are priceless treasures offered from your Heavenly Father. Use them. After all, an obvious way to say "thank you" to the Giver is to use the gifts He has given.

You are the only person on earth
who can use your ability.
Zig Ziglar

One thing taught large in the Holy Scriptures
is that while God gives His gifts freely,
He will require a strict accounting of them at
the end of the road. Each man is personally
responsible for his store, be it large or small,
and will be required to explain his use of it
before the judgment seat of Christ.
A. W. Tozer

In the great orchestra we call life, you have
an instrument and a song, and you owe it
to God to play them both sublimely.
Max Lucado

Each man has his own gift from God;
one has this gift, another has that.
1 Corinthians 7:7 NIV

A Prayer for the Journey

Lord, You have given all of us talents,
and I am no exception. You have blessed me
with a gift—let me discover it, nurture it,
and use it to the glory of Your Kingdom. Today,
let me be a good and faithful steward, Father,
of my talents and my possessions. Let me
share my gifts with the world, and let me offer
praise to You, the Giver of all things good.
— Amen —

The Cheerful Giver

So let each one give as he purposes
in his heart, not grudgingly or of necessity;
for God loves a cheerful giver.
2 Corinthians 9:7 NKJV

The thread of generosity is woven—completely and inextricably—into the very fabric of Christ's teachings. As He sent His disciples out to heal the sick and spread God's message of salvation, Jesus offered this guiding principle: "Freely you have received, freely give" (Matthew 10:8 NIV). The principle still applies. If we are to be disciples of Christ, we must give freely of our time, our possessions, and our love.

In 2 Corinthians 9, Paul reminds us that when we sow the seeds of generosity, we reap bountiful rewards in accordance with God's plan for our lives. Thus, we are instructed to give cheerfully and without reservation because "God loves a cheerful giver" (v. 7).

Today, make this pledge and keep it: Be a cheerful, generous, courageous giver. The world needs your help, and you need the spiritual rewards that will be yours when you do.

Do things for others and you'll find your
self-consciousness evaporating like morning
dew on a Missouri cornfield in July.
Dale Carnegie

There is no happiness in having,
or in getting, but only in giving.
Henry Drummond

We must not only give what we have,
we must also give what we are.
Désiré Joseph Mercier

The righteous give without sparing.
Proverbs 21:26 NIV

A Prayer for the Journey

Lord, You have blessed me with a love that
is far beyond my limited understanding.
You loved me before I was ever born; You sent
Your Son Jesus to redeem me from my sins;
You have given me the gift of eternal life.
Let me be thankful always, and let me praise
You always. Today, let me share priceless
blessings I have received: Let me share my
joy, my possessions, and my faith with others.
And let me be a cheerful giver, Lord,
so that all the glory might be Yours.
— Amen —

Hard Work for the Journey

The plans of the diligent lead to profit
as surely as haste leads to poverty.
Proverbs 21:5 NIV

Now that graduation is a not-too-distant memory, it's time to relax and celebrate . . . for a while. Then, it's time to move on to your next grand adventure. Wherever that adventure may lead, be forewarned: Success will depend, in large part, upon the quality and quantity of your work.

God has created a world in which diligence is rewarded and sloth is not. So whatever it is that you choose to do, do it with commitment, excitement, and vigor. Your boss is watching . . . and so is God.

Think enthusiastically about everything,
especially your work.
Norman Vincent Peale

The higher the ideal, the more work
is required to accomplish it. Do not expect
to become a great success in life if you
are not willing to work for it.
Father Flanagan

An idle life and a holy heart
are a contradiction.
Thomas Brooks

But as for you, be strong and do not give up,
for your work will be rewarded.
2 Chronicles 15:7 NIV

A Prayer for the Journey

Heavenly Father, I seek to be Your faithful
servant. When I am tired, give me strength.
When I become frustrated, give me patience.
When I lose sight of Your purpose for my life,
give me a passion for my daily responsibilities,
and when I have completed my work,
let all the honor and glory be Yours.
— Amen —

God's Strength
for the Journey

Come to me, all you who are weary
and burdened, and I will give you rest.
Take my yoke upon you and learn from me,
for I am gentle and humble in heart, and you
will find rest for your souls. For my yoke
is easy and my burden is light.

Matthew 11:28-30 NIV

God is an unending source of strength and courage if we call upon Him. When we are weary, He gives us strength. When we see no hope, God reminds us of His promises. When we grieve, God wipes away our tears.

Do you feel overwhelmed by today's responsibilities? Do you feel pressured by the ever-increasing demands of 21st-century life? Then turn your concerns and your prayers over to God. He knows your needs, and He has promised to meet those needs. Whatever your circumstances, God will protect you and care for you . . . if you let Him. Invite Him into your heart and allow Him to renew your spirits. When you trust Him and Him alone, He will never fail you.

God gives us always strength enough,
and sense enough,
for everything He wants us to do.
John Ruskin

Jesus is not a strong man making men and
women who gather around Him weak.
He is the Strong creating the strong.
E. Stanley Jones

God walks with us. He scoops us up in
His arms or simply sits with us in silent
strength until we cannot avoid the awesome
recognition that yes, even now, He is here.
Gloria Gaither

I can do all things through Christ
which strengtheneth me.
Philippians 4:13 KJV

A Prayer for the Journey

Dear Heavenly Father, You are my strength
and my protector. When I am troubled, You
comfort me. When I am discouraged, You lift
me up. When I am afraid, You deliver me.
Let me turn to You, Lord, when I am weak.
In times of adversity, let me trust Your plan,
Lord, and whatever my circumstances, let me
look to You for my strength and my salvation.

— Amen —

A Time for Worship

I was glad when they said unto me,
Let us go into the house of the LORD.

Psalm 122:1 KJV

Everyone is engaged in the practice of worship. Some choose to worship God and, as a result, reap the joy that He intends for His children. Others distance themselves from God by worshiping such things as earthly possessions or personal gratification . . . and when they do so, they suffer.

Today, make every aspect of your life a cause for celebration and worship. Praise God for the blessings and opportunities that He has given you, and live according to the beautiful words found in the fifth chapter of 1 Thessalonians: "Rejoice evermore. Pray without ceasing. In every thing give thanks: for this is the will of God in Christ Jesus concerning you" (16-18). God deserves your worship, your prayers, your praise, and your thanks. And, you deserve the joy that is yours when you worship Him with your prayers, your deeds, and your life.

Worship is not taught from the pulpit.
It must be learned in the heart.
Jim Elliot

I am of the opinion that we should not be
concerned about working for God until
we have learned the meaning and delight
of worshiping Him.
A.W. Tozer

Spiritual worship comes from our very core
and is fueled by an awesome reverence
and desire for God.
Beth Moore

Happy are those who hear the joyful call
to worship, for they will walk in the light
of your presence, LORD.
Psalm 89:15 NLT

A Prayer for the Journey

Heavenly Father, this world can be a place
of distractions and temptations. But when I
worship You, Lord, You direct my path and
You cleanse my heart. Let today and every day
be a time of worship and praise. Let me
worship You in everything that I think and do.
Thank You, Father, for the priceless gift of
Your Son Jesus. Let me be worthy of that gift,
and let me give You the praise
and the glory forever.
— Amen —

A Humble Spirit

Humble yourselves, therefore,
under God's mighty hand,
that he may lift you up in due time.
1 Peter 5:6 NIV

Dietrich Bonhoeffer observed, "It is very easy to overestimate the importance of our own achievements in comparison with what we owe others." How true. Even those of us who consider ourselves "self-made" men and women are deeply indebted to more people than we can count. Our first and greatest indebtedness, of course, is to God and His only begotten Son. But we are also indebted to ancestors, parents, teachers, friends, spouses, family members, coworkers, fellow believers . . . and the list goes on.

With so many people who rightfully deserve to share the credit for our successes, how can we gloat? The answer, of course, is that we should not.

As a recent graduate, you have successfully completed an important chapter in your life. You are entitled to take pride in your accomplishments. But not too much pride. Instead of puffing out your chest and saying, "Look at me!", give credit where credit is due, starting with God. And rest assured: There is no such thing as a self-made man. All of us are made by God . . . and He deserves the glory, not us.

We are never stronger than
the moment we admit we are weak.
Beth Moore

It was pride that changed angels into devils;
it is humility that makes men as angels.
St. Augustine

A humble heart is like a magnet
that draws the favor of God toward us.
Jim Cymbala

Don't be selfish . . . . Be humble,
thinking of others as better than yourself.
Philippians 2:3 NLT

A Prayer for the Journey

Heavenly Father, Jesus clothed Himself with
humility when He chose to leave heaven and
come to earth to live and die for all creation.
Christ is my Master and my example.
Clothe me with humility, Lord, so that
I might be more like Your Son.
— Amen —

Stillness
Before God

Be still, and know that I am God.
Psalm 46:10 KJV

We live in a fast-paced world. The demands of everyday life can seem overwhelming at times, but when we slow ourselves down and seek the presence of a loving God, we invite His peace into our hearts.

Do you set aside quiet moments each day to offer praise to your Creator? You should. During these moments of stillness, you will often sense the infinite love and power of our Lord.

The familiar words of Psalm 46:10 remind us to "Be still, and know that I am God." When we do so, we encounter the awesome presence of our loving Heavenly Father, and we are comforted in the knowledge that God is not just near. He is here.

Most of man's trouble comes from
his inability to be still.
Blaise Pascal

Ten minutes spent in Christ's society
every day, aye two minutes,
will make the whole day different.
Henry Drummond

Let this be your chief object in prayer,
to realize the presence of your Heavenly
Father. Let your watchword be:
Alone with God.
Andrew Murray

In quietness and in confidence
shall be your strength.
Isaiah 30:15 KJV

A Prayer for the Journey

Lord, Your Holy Word is a light unto the world;
let me study it, trust it, and share it with all
who cross my path. Let me discover You,
Father, in the quiet moments of the day. And,
in all that I say and do, help me to be a worthy
witness as I share the Good News of
Your perfect Son and Your perfect Word.

— Amen —

A Time for Forgiveness

And be kind to one another, tenderhearted,
forgiving one another,
just as God in Christ forgave you.
Ephesians 4:32 NKJV

Forgiveness is God's commandment, but oh how difficult a commandment it can be to follow. Being frail, fallible, imperfect human beings, we are quick to anger, quick to blame, slow to forgive, and even slower to forget. No matter. Forgiveness, no matter how difficult, is God's way, and it must be our way, too.

God's commandments are not intended to be customized for the particular whims of particular believers. Far from it. God's Holy Word is a book that must be taken in its entirety; all of God's commandments are to be taken seriously. And, so it is with forgiveness.

If, in your heart, you hold bitterness against even a single person, forgive. If there exists even one person, alive or dead, whom you have not forgiven, follow God's commandment and His will for your life: forgive. If you are embittered against yourself for some past mistake or shortcoming, forgive. Then, to the best of your abilities, forget. And move on. Hatred and bitterness and regret are not part of God's plan for your life. Forgiveness is.

What makes a Christian a Christian
is not perfection but forgiveness.
Max Lucado

Learning how to forgive and forget is one of
the secrets of a happy Christian life.
Warren Wiersbe

Forgiveness is the key that unlocks the door
of resentment and the handcuffs of hate. It is
a power that breaks the chains of bitterness
and the shackles of selfishness.
Corrie ten Boom

For if you forgive men when they sin against
you, your heavenly Father will also forgive
you. But if you do not forgive men their sins,
your Father will not forgive your sins.
Matthew 6:14-15 NIV

A Prayer for the Journey

Dear Lord, when I am bitter, You can change
my unforgiving heart. When I am slow
to forgive, Your Word reminds me that
forgiveness is Your commandment. Let me
be Your obedient servant, Lord, and let me
forgive others just as You have forgiven me.
— Amen —

A Prayer for Perseverance

Let us not become weary in doing good,
for at the proper time we will reap
a harvest if we do not give up.
Galatians 6:9 NIV

Now that you've graduated, the hard work is over . . . right? Wrong! Even if you have worked very hard in school, there is still more work to do . . . much more work. In fact, the most challenging years of your life are probably still ahead, so prepare yourself. And learn to be patient.

Our Savior, Christ Jesus, finished what He began. Despite the torture He endured, despite the shame of the cross, Jesus was steadfast in His faithfulness to God. We, too, must remain faithful, especially during times of hardship and pain.

Perhaps you are in a hurry for God to reveal His plans for your life. If so, be forewarned: God operates on His own timetable, not yours. Sometimes, God may answer your prayers with silence, and when He does, you must patiently persevere. In times of trouble, seek God through prayer and lean upon His strength. Whatever your problem, He can handle it. Your job is to keep persevering until He does.

Stand still and refuse to retreat. Look at it as God looks at it and draw upon His power to hold up under the blast.
Charles Swindoll

In the Bible, patience is not a passive acceptance of circumstances. It is a courageous perseverance in the face of suffering and difficulty.
Warren Wiersbe

Jesus taught that perseverance is the essential element in prayer.
E. M. Bounds

Those who hope in the LORD will renew their strength. They will soar on wings like eagles; they will run and not grow weary, they will walk and not be faint.
Isaiah 40:31 NIV

A Prayer for the Journey

Lord, when times are tough, I am tempted
to give up. But You are my God, and I can
draw strength from You. When I am exhausted,
You energize me. When I am afraid, You give
me courage. You are with me, God,
in good times and in bad, and I will praise
You with perseverance and
with trust in my heart for You.

— Amen —

When Our Hearts Are Heavy

Blessed are those who mourn,
for they will be comforted.
Matthew 5:4 NIV

All of us experience adversity and pain. When we lose something—or someone—we love, we grieve our losses. When we lose a loved one, or when we experience any other profound loss, darkness overwhelms us for a while, and it seems as if we cannot summon the strength to face another day—but, with God's help, we can.

When our friends or family members encounter life-shattering events, we struggle to find words that might offer them comfort and support. But finding the right words can be difficult, if not impossible. Sometimes, all that we can do is to be with our loved ones, offering them few words but much love.

Thankfully, God promises that He is "close to the brokenhearted" (Psalm 34:18 NIV). In times of intense sadness, we must turn to Him, and we must encourage our friends and family members to do likewise. When we do, our Father comforts us and, in time, He heals us.

You who suffer take heart.
Christ is the answer to sorrow.
Billy Graham

Even in the winter, even in the midst of
the storm, the sun is still there. Somewhere,
up above the clouds, it still shines and warms
and pulls at the life buried deep inside
the brown branches and frozen earth.
The sun is there! Spring will come.
Gloria Gaither

When all else is gone, God is still left.
Nothing changes Him.
Hannah Whitall Smith

When I sit in darkness,
the LORD shall be a light unto me.
Micah 7:8 KJV

A Prayer for the Journey

Heavenly Father, Your Word promises that
You will not give us more than we can bear;
You have promised to lift us out of our grief
and despair. Today, Lord, I pray for those who
mourn, and I thank You for sustaining all of us
in our days of sorrow. May we trust You
always and praise You forever.

— Amen —

Wisdom for the Journey

For the LORD gives wisdom,
and from his mouth come knowledge
and understanding.
Proverbs 2:6 NIV

Now that you've graduated, your head is undoubtedly filled with valuable information. But, there is much yet to learn. Wisdom is like a savings account: If you add to it consistently, then eventually you'll have a great sum. The secret to success is consistency.

Do you seek wisdom? Then keep learning. Seek wisdom every day, and seek it in the right place. That place, of course, is, first and foremost, the Word of God. When you study God's Word and live according to His commandments, you will surely become wise, and because of your wisdom, you will be blessed by your Father in heaven.

If you lack knowledge, go to school.
If you lack wisdom, get on your knees.
Vance Havner

Knowledge is horizontal. Wisdom is vertical;
it comes down from above.
Billy Graham

Patience is the companion of wisdom.
St. Augustine

I will instruct you and teach you in
the way you should go; I will counsel you
and watch over you.
Psalm 32:8 NIV

A Prayer for the Journey

Lord, when I trust in the wisdom of the world,
I will sometimes be led astray, but when I trust
in Your wisdom, I build my life on a firm
foundation. Today and every day I will trust
Your Word and follow it, knowing that
the ultimate wisdom is Your wisdom
and the ultimate truth is Your truth.

— Amen —

The Journey
Beyond Worry

Therefore do not worry about tomorrow,
for tomorrow will worry about itself.
Each day has enough trouble of its own.

Matthew 6:34 NIV

Because we are fallible human beings, we worry. Even though we, as Christians, have the assurance of salvation—even though we have the promise of God's love and protection—we find ourselves fretting over the countless details of everyday life. Jesus understood our concerns when He spoke the reassuring words found in the sixth chapter of Matthew.

Perhaps you are concerned about the inevitable changes that have come as a result of your graduation. Perhaps you are uncertain about your future or your finances. Or perhaps you are simply a "worrier" by nature. If so, make Matthew 6 a regular part of your daily Bible reading. This beautiful passage will remind you that God still sits in His heaven and you are His beloved child. Then, perhaps, you will worry a little less and trust God a little more, and that's as it should be because God is trustworthy . . . and you are protected.

Worry does not empty tomorrow of its sorrow;
it empties today of its strength.
Corrie ten Boom

Remember always that there are two things
which are more utterly incompatible even
than oil and water, and these two are
trust and worry.
Hannah Whitall Smith

Pray, and let God worry.
Martin Luther

Let not your heart be troubled:
ye believe in God, believe also in me.
John 14:1 KJV

A Prayer for the Journey

Lord, sometimes, I can't seem to help myself:
I worry. Even though I know to put my trust in
You, I still become anxious about the future.
Give me the wisdom to trust in You,
Father, and give me the courage to live
a life of faith, not a life of fear.
— Amen —

A Life of Truth

Jesus answered, "I am the way and
the truth and the life. No one comes to
the Father except through me."
John 14:6 NIV

As the familiar saying goes, "Honesty is the best policy." For believers, it is far more important to note that honesty is God's policy. And if we are to be servants worthy of our Savior, Jesus Christ, we must be honest and forthright in our communications with others.

Sometimes, honesty is difficult; sometimes, honesty is painful; but always honesty is God's commandment. In the Book of Exodus, God did not command, "Thou shalt not bear false witness when it is convenient." God said, "Thou shalt not bear false witness against thy neighbor." Period.

Sometime soon, perhaps even today, you will be tempted to bend the truth or perhaps even break it. Resist that temptation. Truth is God's way, and it must also be yours. Period.

Truth will triumph. The Father of truth
will win, and the followers of truth
will be saved.
Max Lucado

Learning God's truth and getting it into our
heads is one thing, but *living* God's truth
and getting it into our characters
is quite something else.
Warren Wiersbe

Those who walk in truth walk in liberty.
Beth Moore

The sum of Your word is truth, and every one
of Your righteous ordinances is everlasting.
Psalm 119:160 NASB

A Prayer for the Journey

Dear Lord, Jesus said He was the truth,
and I believe Him. Father, may Jesus always
be the standard for truth in my life so that
I might be a worthy example to others
and a worthy servant to You.

— Amen —

Patience for the Journey

Be completely humble and gentle; be patient,
bearing with one another in love.

Ephesians 4:2 NIV

Life demands patience . . . and lots of it! We live in an imperfect world inhabited by imperfect people. Sometimes, we inherit troubles from others, and sometimes we create trouble for ourselves. In either case, what's required is patience.

Lamentations 3:25-26 reminds us that, "The LORD is wonderfully good to those who wait for him and seek him. So it is good to wait quietly for salvation from the LORD" (NIV). But, for most of us, waiting quietly for God is difficult. Why? Because we are fallible human beings, sometimes quick to anger and sometimes slow to forgive.

The next time you find your patience tested to the limit, remember that the world unfolds according to God's timetable, not ours. Sometimes, we must wait patiently, and that's as it should be. After all, think how patient God has been with us.

Let me encourage you to continue to wait
with faith. God may not perform a miracle,
but He is trustworthy to touch you and
make you whole where there used to be a hole.
Lisa Whelchel

The next time you're disappointed,
don't panic and don't give up. Just be patient
and let God remind you he's still in control.
Max Lucado

All things pass. Patience attains
all it strives for.
St. Teresa of Avila

Rejoice in hope; be patient in affliction;
be persistent in prayer.
Romans 12:12 HCSB

A Prayer for the Journey

Heavenly Father, give me patience.
Let me live according to Your plan and
according to Your timetable. When I am
hurried, slow me down. When I become
impatient with others, give me empathy. When
I am frustrated by the demands of the day,
give me peace. Today, let me be a patient
Christian, Dear Lord, as I trust in You
and in Your master plan for my life.
— Amen —

Celebrating the Journey

This is the day which the LORD has made;
let us rejoice and be glad in it.
Psalm 118:24 NASB

G raduation spells the beginning of a new chapter in your life. You have every reason to be excited. But remember: The coming chapter, like every other, begins and ends with God and with His Son.

God will touch your heart and guide your steps .... if you let Him. So, dedicate this day to God's purpose and give thanks for His grace. This is the day the Lord has created—give thanks to the One who created it, and use it to the glory of His kingdom.

All our life is a celebration for us;
we are convinced, in fact, that God is always
everywhere. We sing while we work . . .
we pray while we carry out all life's
other occupations.
St. Clement of Alexandria

God can take any man and
put the miracle of His joy into him.
Oswald Chambers

The greatest honor you can give Almighty God
is to live gladly and joyfully because
of the knowledge of His love.
Juliana of Norwich

Rejoice in the Lord always.
I will say it again: Rejoice!
Philippians 4:4 HCSB

A Prayer for the Journey

Lord, Your desire is that I be complete in
Your joy. Joy begets celebration. Today,
I celebrate the life and work You have given
me, and I celebrate the lives of my friends
and family. Thank You, Father, for Your love,
for Your blessings, and for Your joy.
Let me treasure Your gifts and share
them this day and forever.
— Amen —

A Prayer for the Journey

Jesus said to them, "I am the bread of life;
he who comes to Me will not hunger,
and he who believes in Me will never thirst.
John 6:35 NASB

As you take the next steps in your journey, remember to take those steps with God. And remember to pray.

Is prayer an integral part of your daily life or is it a hit-or-miss habit? Do you "pray without ceasing," or is your prayer life an afterthought? Remember: the quality of your spiritual life will be in direct proportion to the quality of your prayer life.

Prayer changes things and it changes you. Today, instead of turning things over in your mind, turn them over to God in prayer. Instead of worrying about your next decision, decide to let God lead the way. Don't limit your prayers to meals or to bedtime. Pray constantly about things great and small. God is listening, and He wants to hear from you now.

Some people pray just to pray,
and some people pray to know God.
Andrew Murray

Prayer does not change God; it changes me.
C. S. Lewis

Those who know God the best are
the richest and the most powerful in prayer.
Little acquaintance with God makes prayer
a rare and feeble thing.
E. M. Bounds

For the eyes of the Lord are over the righteous,
and his ears are open unto their prayers:
but the face of the Lord is against
them that do evil.
1 Peter 3:12 KJV

A Prayer for the Journey

Dear Lord, when I pray, let me feel
Your presence. When I worship You,
let me feel Your love. In the quiet moments of
the day, I will open my heart to You, Almighty
God. And I know that You are with me always
and that You will hear my prayers.

— Amen —

Thoughts for Your Journey

Using God's Gifts

Neglect not the gift that is in thee . . . .
1 Timothy 4:14 KJV

You need to understand that you are being
influenced by selfish pride when you reject
the gifts of God just because they do not come
in a shape that suits your taste.
Fénelon

Bless the LORD, O my soul, and
forget not all his benefits . . . .
Psalm 103:2 KJV

Every good gift and every perfect gift is from above, and cometh down from the Father of lights.

—

James 1:17 KJV

Spiritual Abundance

Success, success to you, and success to those
who help you, for your God is with you . . . .
1 Chronicles 12:18 NIV

People, places, and things were never meant
to give us life. God alone
is the author of a fulfilling life.
Gary Smalley & John Trent

Have faith in the Lord your God and you
will be upheld; have faith in his prophets and
you will be successful.
2 Chronicles 20:20 NIV

Delight thyself also in the LORD;
and he shall give thee
the desires of thine heart.

—

Psalm 37:4 KJV

God's Will

Teach me to do thy will;
for thou art my God: thy Spirit is good;
lead me into the land of uprightness.
Psalm 143:10 KJV

The will of God is a living relationship
between God and the believer.
Warren Wiersbe

Father, if it be possible, let this cup pass
from me: nevertheless, not as I will,
but as thou wilt.
Matthew 26:39 KJV

For whosoever shall do the will
of my Father which is in heaven,
the same is my brother,
and sister, and mother.

—

Matthew 12:50 KJV

God's Timing

He has made everything beautiful in its time.
He has also set eternity in the hearts of men;
yet they cannot fathom what God
has done from beginning to end.
Ecclesiastes 3:11 NIV

God has a designated time when
his promise will be fulfilled and
the prayer will be answered.
Jim Cymbala

And we know that in all things God works
for the good of those who love him, who have
been called according to his purpose.
Romans 8:28 NIV

There is a time for everything,
and a season for
every activity under heaven . . . .

—

Ecclesiastes 3:1 NIV

Encouraging Others

Take heed, brethren, lest there be
in any of you an evil heart of unbelief,
in departing from the living God. But exhort
one another daily, while it is called Today;
lest any of you be hardened through
the deceitfulness of sin.
Hebrews 3:12-13 KJV

Encouragement is the oxygen of the soul.
John Maxwell

Do not let any unwholesome talk come out
of your mouths, but only what is helpful for
building others up according to their needs,
that it may benefit those who listen.
Ephesians 4:29 NIV

Let us consider how to stimulate
one another to love and good deeds.

—

Hebrews 10:24 KJV

On Faith

But he must ask in faith without any doubting,
for the one who doubts is like the surf
of the sea, driven and tossed by the wind.
James 1:6 NASB

Prayer is the key to Heaven,
but faith unlocks the door.
Mosie Lister

Be on the alert, stand firm in the faith,
act like men, be strong.
1 Corinthians 16:13 NASB

For the LORD watches over
the way of the righteous, but
the way of the wicked will perish.

—

Psalm 1:6 NIV

Forgiving Others

A man's wisdom gives him patience;
it is to his glory to overlook an offense.
Proverbs 19:11 NIV

Sometimes, we need a housecleaning
of the heart.
Catherine Marshall

Then came Peter to him, and said, Lord,
how oft shall my brother sin against me, and
I forgive him? till seven times? Jesus saith
unto him, I say not unto thee, Until seven
times: but, Until seventy times seven.
Matthew 18:21-22 KJV

Blessed are the merciful:
for they shall obtain mercy.

—

Matthew 5:7 KJV

Thanks to God

I will thank you, Lord with all my heart;
I will tell of all the marvelous things you have
done. I will be filled with joy because of you.
I will sing praises to your name, O Most High.
Psalm 9:1-2 NLT

Praise and thank God for who He is
and for what He has done for you.
Billy Graham

Give thanks in all circumstances;
for this is God's will for you in Christ Jesus.
1 Thessalonians 5:18 NIV

All Your works shall give thanks
to You, O LORD,
And Your godly ones
shall bless You.

—

Psalm 145:10 NASB